# WORDS OF CHANGE
# BODY

# WORDS
# OF CHANGE

# BODY

## POWERFUL VOICES,
## INSPIRING IDEAS

### MAIYSHA KAI

SPRUCE BOOKS
A Sasquatch Books Imprint

FOR EVERY BODY . . .
IN HOPES THAT YOU
FIND YOURSELF AT
HOME THERE

I can't give people
permission to see me
as my body.

—BEANIE FELDSTEIN

# INTRODUCTION

**W**hat is the story you tell about your body?

Is it a romance or a sprawling, multigenerational history? A revealing memoir or a mystery? Do you consider it a divine comedy or a tragedy of epic proportions? The stories we tell about our bodies—how they look, the purposes they serve, and how we should feel about them—is . . . complicated. And if we're honest, more often than not, we cast our bodies not as our trusty sidekicks, but rather as our nemeses.

Our stories begin with our bodies. We base our plotlines—and our judgments—on the whims of the genetic lottery that determined our biological gender characteristics, skin color, size, shape, facial features, physical abilities, and even hair texture. Whether we love them, tolerate them, celebrate them, fear them, or loathe them, our relationship with our bodies is the most enduring and intense of our lives. A relationship that is more intimate than our bonds with our closest family, friends, and partners. Most of us wouldn't willingly spend time with a nemesis. We certainly wouldn't want to be tethered to them for a lifetime.

Intellectually, we know we are more than the sum of our parts. Emotionally, we are not so sure. How can we be, when daily, we are bombarded with images and messages dictating how we should look, what we should buy, and how we should live? The assumed preference for slim, symmetrical, cisgender, nondisabled, shapely, toned, and predominantly white, young bodies is both inescapable and an ever-moving goalpost—by design. Yes, the bulk of the messaging is driven by advertisers' and retailers' profit motives. But even our friends and family, vulnerable to these same messages, may add their voices to the chorus, not-so-subtly reinforcing the idea that these attributes are aspirational, if not ideal.

What story would you tell about your body if no one was telling you otherwise?

If I were to tell the story of my body, it might have all the makings of an epic war saga—or perhaps a tortured romance. For decades, my body and I have remained locked in a love-hate relationship: the kind of "will they or won't they?" tension that keeps readers on the edge of their seats. While my body and I may have currently reached a tenuous and perhaps temporary truce, so far we have battled through puberty, an eating disorder, countless heartbreaks and even more diets, massive weight fluctuations, self-destructive behavior, institutional and overt racism and sexism—and with every passing day, age.

There's even more to the tale: My tall, Black, female, cisgender, curvy, olive-complected, nondisabled body and I have spent decades inside what is called the "beauty industrial complex"—first as a "plus-size" model, and currently as a beauty and fashion editor. In that space, I have had a front-row seat to the unique privileges, messaging, and often humiliating commodification of beauty. As part of a generation of models who pushed for the inclusion of (marginally) bigger bodies, I'm proud that my story includes having an active role in dismantling some of the status quo and building in its place what we now know as the body positivity movement. I also know we haven't come nearly far enough.

Worse, we can even be part of the problem.

The term "body-positive" has become trendy in recent years, but the rhetoric still fails to fully reflect reality. In spite of its all-inclusive ethos, fat-phobia, ageism, racism, colorism, ableism, and transphobia all continue to plague our collective consciousness, as well as our understanding and acceptance of ourselves. As a result, *who* gets to be positive about their bodies—and at what cost—are questions yet to be fully answered.

Many seats at the table are still waiting to be filled, voices yet to be heard, stories still untold. This book presents a range of those voices— some well-known and others less so. Their stories, musings, and revelations about our incredible, often unpredictable, constant companions we call bodies express love, appreciation, frustration, empathy, awe, vulnerability, righteous indignation, and vindication. Many of those included in this collection speak in first person, and that's not accidental.

When it comes to the stories of our bodies, it's personal. And while our bodies may be individual, body issues are universal. I hope you'll approach this book with similar openness to the story your body has to tell, because if you're reading this, that story is still unfinished.

Let's write the next chapter with curiosity, acceptance, and love.

Maiysha Kai

I don't think of body shaming. You can't shame me. I'm aware of my weight and the way the world might perceive it. . . . But I don't let it affect me. It does not affect my life, it does not make me unhappy. I tackle it the way that I can. It is a part of me, but I am not a victim of my weight.

—ANDRÉ LEON TALLEY

"

FOR BLACK WOMEN,
IT'S NEVER BEEN 'JUST
HAIR.' IT'S LINKED TO OUR
IDENTITY, CULTURE, AND
CREATIVE EXPRESSION. . . .
OUR HAIR ALSO ALLOWS
US TO SHAPE-SHIFT,
GLIDE FROM ONE SPACE
TO THE NEXT.

—AMA KWARTENG

"

"I don't have a twenty-
year-old's body any longer.
You come to terms with it.
It's just gravity, baby."

—LYNDA CARTER

"We don't change. We take the gravel and the shell and we make a pearl. And we help other people to change so that they can see more kinds of beauty."

—P!NK

The topic of body positivity isn't gender-specific. . . . Men need to be included in the conversation that's being had. . . . A large part of body positivity has to do with mental health, and the consistent lack of diverse male body representation in the media and social media is creating a true epidemic.

—ANTHONY PATRICK MANIERI

"I LOVE MY BODY
AND I'M STILL FAT.
I'M BEAUTIFUL
AND I'M STILL FAT.
THESE THINGS ARE
NOT MUTUALLY
EXCLUSIVE."

—LIZZO

"I still feel pressured to look a certain way. . . . Just because I've lost weight doesn't mean that I'm happy and content with my body. Because of the media, and because of what I feel I should look like, it's always going to be a battle in my head."

—SAM SMITH

# "

IT'S UNQUESTIONABLY
BETTER FOR EVERYONE
TO SEE A VARIETY OF
BODY TYPES, AGES, AND
ETHNICITIES, RATHER
THAN A SINGLE IDEALIZED
VERSION OF A WOMAN. . . .
WHO COULD ARGUE WITH
THAT MESSAGE?

—LINDA WELLS

"

"TODAY, I AM A FAT
WOMAN. I DON'T THINK
I AM UGLY. I DON'T HATE
MYSELF IN THE WAY
SOCIETY WOULD HAVE
ME HATE MYSELF, BUT
. . . I HATE HOW THE
WORLD ALL TOO OFTEN
RESPONDS TO THIS BODY."

—ROXANE GAY

"The beauty myth—an obsession
with physical perfection that traps
modern women in an endless cycle
of hopelessness, self-consciousness,
and self-hatred as she tries to fulfill
society's impossible definition of
flawless beauty."

—SELENA GOMEZ

# HAVING A DISABILITY HAS SHOWN ME THAT I HAVE THIS SORT OF LIKE GREAT ABILITY TO ADAPT TO ANY ENVIRONMENT.

—MAMA CAX

European standards of beauty are something that plague the entire world— the idea that darker skin is not beautiful, that light skin is the key to success and love. . . . This is the message: that dark skin is unacceptable.

—LUPITA NYONG'O

"It annoys me whenever I hear people talking about 'body image' and they're only banging on about how much they love their appearance. Fair play to them. I'm jealous. Because I don't like the way I look. I'm not comfortable in my skin and perhaps I never truly will be. And, to be honest, I don't think I'm the only one. When I say this to other men, most of them tell me they feel the same, so why don't we talk about this stuff more openly?"

—DAVE CHAWNER

"WOKE UP
THIS MORNING
WITH MY MIND SET
ON LOVING ME."

—JAMILA WOODS

"Instead of viewing an arch—
you rise, you peak, you decline—
view it as a staircase. . . . Your body
may fall apart, but on every level
that really matters, you can ascend
toward enlightenment, wisdom,
and authenticity."

—JANE FONDA

# "

IN AN IDEAL WORLD,
I WOULDN'T HAVE TO
CHANGE MY BODY.
I WOULDN'T HAVE TO
DO ALL THIS STUFF.
I WOULDN'T HAVE
TO BE PRETTY, OR
'FEMININE' AND PEOPLE
WOULD RESPECT THAT.

—HARI NEF

"

If my body could talk,
it would say *SHOW ME TO
PEOPLE! Show them you're
proud of me, show them how
beautiful we are, show them
they don't have to prefer a
body type to show respect to
the person in that body.
Show them all.*

—LILLIAN BUSTLE

"Just realize, like, it's perfect.
Your body is perfect and it doesn't
matter, a chunk here and a fat
here and a cellulite here and your
stomach this or that. That shit is
just such a waste of time."

—ALEX BORSTEIN

"Just because we fight for women's rights doesn't mean we shouldn't have anything to do with sexuality. . . . I'm not ashamed of my body."

—WARIS DIRIE

"IF A BOY CAN OPEN
UP A MAGAZINE OR A
READ A BLOG OR WATCH
TV AND SEE A BIGGER
GUY WHO REMINDS THEM
OF THEMSELVES BEING
TOUTED AS DESIRABLE . . .
THAT WOULD HAVE DONE
WONDERS FOR MY SELF-
ESTEEM AS A LITTLE KID."

—ZACH MIKO

"Fat bodies are vast and textured, much like the oceans that stretch out from the land."

—SHOOG McDANIEL

"YOU HAVE TO GET UP
AND BECOME YOUR OWN
WORK OF ART; FROM
THE MOMENT YOU PUT
YOURSELF TOGETHER . . .
CELEBRATE WHO YOU ARE
AND CELEBRATE LIFE AND
KNOW THAT THIS IS
YOUR EXPERIENCE."

—SALMA HAYEK

"The real difference isn't
my skin. It's the fact that
I don't find my beauty in
the opinions of others. I'm
beautiful because I know it."

—WINNIE HARLOW

"

I was my first tormentor, eager
to hate my body as much as I
believed the world did. This
hatred was a thing that the world
and I had in common. The enemy
of my enemy is my friend, as the
saying goes. I knew hatred and
self-pity like the back of my hand;
we moved in sync, like a carefully
choreographed dance routine.

—KEAH BROWN

"

"Apparently, if you believe social media, a Black person is supposed to have [a] skinny waist, flat stomach, booty on fat-fat, big boobies, and a 3C curl and in my head, I'm like: 'But I don't look like that. No one around me looks like that. . . . What does *Black features* even mean?'"

—PHILOMENA KWAO

I am very aware that I am
an African American female
who is curvy, who is over size ten,
so it is imperative to me that our
television and our movies reflect
the reality of our world—that's
what I'm desperately in pursuit of.
For me, an action movie—
a genuine action movie that is not
comical or commenting on the
actor's size but where she is really
kicking butt as a curvy girl—
is so cool.

—Da'VINE JOY RANDOLPH

"I understood very quickly, even as a thirteen-year-old, that if I were to express myself sexually I would feel unsafe. . . . I felt the need to cover my body and to inhibit my expression and my work in order to send my own message to the world that I'm someone worth[y] of safety and respect."

—NATALIE PORTMAN

"It doesn't matter what size you are—it's how big you are as a human being that really matters. You can have a skinny ass and still have a fat head."

—DOLLY PARTON

# "WE ALL HAVE BODIES— SOME ARE BIGGER, SOME ARE SMALLER, SOME HAVE SCARS."

—JAZZ JENNINGS

"What if I told you disability is something society created? By putting up barriers to inclusion and negative preconceptions. . . . I am whole. I am complete. I am disabled by the attitudes of society and the lack of opportunities. I do not have to change anything about my body. Society has to change the way it views my body."

—KELLY KNOX

"WHAT'S FRUSTRATING IS
THAT I WANT TO TELL
PEOPLE JUST HOW HARD
TRAUMA AND SHAME IS, AND
THAT'S WHAT MAKES YOU
UNCOMFORTABLE IN YOUR
SKIN. THAT'S WHAT MAKES
YOU UNHEALTHY, THAT WILL
SHORTEN YOUR LIFE.
THE WEIGHT ITSELF? . . .
WE CAN HOLD IT."

—HANNAH GADSBY

"I really believe everyone has a snapshot of themselves from a time when they were young that they're ashamed of. For me, it's that fourteen-year-old overweight and unattractive kid who felt ugly to the world, who listened to hip hop and wanted so badly to be accepted by this community of skaters."

—JONAH HILL

Starved. It's the perfect word
to describe my experience in a
fat body. . . . A lot of us are not
being sustained in various parts
of our lives because we're told
that we don't deserve *any* form of
sustenance—not the comfort of food
or emotional support or intimacies
or touch, not friendship, not love,
not humanity.

—SHERRONDA J. BROWN

"I DON'T WANNA HAVE
TO TEACH A LESSON ON
HEALTH AT EVERY SIZE
JUST TO GET THROUGH
EVERY CONVERSATION IN
MY DAY. I'M JUST TRYING
TO LIVE MY LIFE."

—SAMANTHA IRBY

"He said to me . . .
'You know what they say: You
are what you eat.' And I turned
around to him [and] went,
'Sorry, mate, but I do not
remember eating a goddess.'"

—JAYDE ADAMS

Who taught you to hate the texture of your hair? Who taught you to hate the color of your skin? . . . Who taught you to hate the shape of your nose and the shape of your lips? Who taught you to hate yourself from the top of your head to the soles of your feet?

—MALCOLM X

"What we now know as trans women is that we are not trying to 'pass'; we are just trying to survive with our lives and our dignity intact. We get caught up in the same struggles that every woman faces, trying to fit our bodies into a box it was never meant to fit into."

—ANGELICA ROSS

There are so many people of the opposite skin tone that get to rise up in the ranks. And the fact that there's so few of us with deeper skin tones, just know there's room for you. . . . Find what you want to say, perfect how you want to say it, and share it with the world because there's an opportunity and there's a space for you.

—NYMA TANG

"I love my butt in a way I
didn't growing up. . . .
I've been—to a certain
extent—at odds with my body
for many years, wanting it
to be something other than
it was, wanting myself to
be something other than I
was. Then . . . I started to get
comfortable with the largeness
of my personality. The same
thing with my butt."

—TRACEE ELLIS ROSS

"ONE IN FIVE PEOPLE
HAVE A DISABILITY,
THAT'S A LOT OF PEOPLE
WHO YOU'RE CHOOSING
NOT TO TALK ABOUT.
THAT IS A MIX OF
VISIBLE AND INVISIBLE
DISABILITIES."

—JILLIAN MERCADO

Stop asking me about my body. . . . Stop picking trans people's bodies apart. . . . Stop asking me questions about my private parts. . . . We are literally still fighting the notion that our lives, [our] humanity, are cosmetic. . . . Don't ask trans people about our bodies without being given consent.

—INDYA MOORE

"Something in our society tells us that women's bodies are fair game for scrutiny in a way that men's simply are not. . . . I hope in the future that more people will talk about our work, our inspirations, our drive, rather than our looks."

—NICOLA COUGHLAN

"

IT'S PRETTY CLEAR
THAT WE'RE ALL
DIFFERENTLY ABLED. NONE
OF US NEED TO BE
LABELED THAT WAY. . . .
THE IDEA OF HOW WE
DESCRIBE OURSELVES
AND OTHERS—ALL OF US—
NEEDS TO EVOLVE.

—AIMEE MULLINS

"

I also need body positivity to mean that Black people are not afraid of being indiscriminately killed during routine traffic stops, because I need to be able to feel positive that my *Black* body is safe in the world. . . . I need trans folk to be able to use the bathroom that identifies with the gender they identify with, because that is part of being positive in *their* bodies. I need mental illness to be destigmatized because *that's* part of being positive in one's body.

—SONYA RENEE TAYLOR

"Don't ever let anyone
tell you how you should
or shouldn't look. There
is no such thing as a
perfect body type."

—ALY RAISMAN

"WE HEAR THE TERM
BODY POSITIVITY ALL THE
TIME. TO BE HONEST,
I DON'T ALWAYS FEEL
POSITIVE ABOUT MY BODY. . . .
I DON'T HAVE TO LIE TO
MYSELF AND TELL MYSELF
I HAVE AN AMAZING BODY.
ALL I HAVE TO SAY IS
'I'M HEALTHY.' IN THAT
STATEMENT, I EXPRESS
GRATITUDE."

—DEMI LOVATO

"IF ME WEARING A BIKINI GOT YOU FEELING SOME TYPE OF WAY YOU HAVE BIGGER PROBLEMS."

—NATASHA ROTHWELL

"I think the perfect image in the fashion industry is that maybe five- to six-year period of time in a woman's life where her skin has no age on it; where she's really the most insecure and she's really the most vulnerable, that they portray as the ideal woman."

—NORMA KAMALI

I remember the day I finally recognized that the biggest hater on my body was, well, me. . . . It sounds a little silly, but sometimes you've gotta be your own hypewoman. . . . We all deserve to be treated better, and reminding myself of that has been incredibly helpful.

—ALLIE FLYNN

"BEAUTIFUL, GROSS,
STRONG, THIN, FAT,
PRETTY, UGLY,
SEXY, DISGUSTING,
FLAWLESS, WOMAN."

—AMY SCHUMER

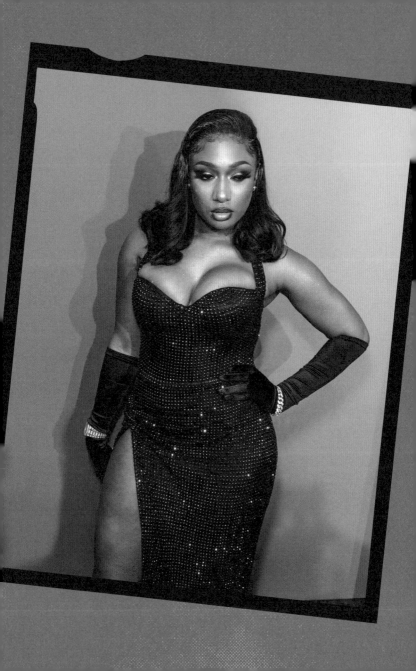

"I love my body. Every curve, every inch, every mark, every dimple is decoration on my temple. My body is mine and nobody owns it but me—and whoever I choose to let in is so lucky. You may not think my body is perfect, and it probably never will be. But when I look in the mirror, I love what I see."

—MEGAN THEE STALLION

"When people put makeup on me to make me look beautiful, it feels strange. I used to wear makeup earlier in my transition. I worked really hard to like my body and face, and now I'm at a point where I don't need makeup in order to feel good about myself."

—HUNTER SCHAFER

"Perhaps you like to torture yourself by trying on some jeans from a few years ago to see if you can button them. Clothes do not exist to humiliate their owners. Please do not force garments into performing psychological tasks for which they were not designed."

—TIM GUNN

# ME AND MY BODY ARE JUST, WE'RE ON A JOURNEY TOGETHER.

## —JESSAMYN STANLEY

"Y'all gotta start normalizing real bodies, okay? Not everybody has a wagon behind them, okay? Guts are normal—they're normal. Boobs sag, *especially* after breastfeeding. Instagram isn't real."

—CHIZI DURU

If I see a kid and he's pointing at me, and the parent has him look the other way, what's that kid going to grow up into? Somebody who can't make eye contact with somebody who's four and a half feet tall? That's sad, to me. . . . But those little things add up in our DNA in terms of how we see people who are physically unique, and that can be destructive.

—PETER DINKLAGE

"I took an African American
studies class at Northwestern
where we explored colorism; it was
the first time I could put a name
to feeling too light in the Black
community, too mixed in the white
community. For castings, I was
labeled 'ethnically ambiguous.'
Was I Latina? Sephardic?
'Exotic Caucasian'?"

—MEGHAN MARKLE

I never saw anyone who looked
quite like me: a tan-skinned
Asian dude of slight build who
grew up fat and lost weight
because he got braces. And
in turn, since I desired these
beautiful men (and assumed
everyone else did) but didn't
look like them, I always thought
no one would desire me.

—MATT ORTILE

"Conventionally pretty people are never asked how they deal with body image, it's just assumed they love their bodies. They are beautiful after all, so why wouldn't they love themselves like we, the world—legitimately and reasonably inside of white supremacy—do? So then the question is always posed to someone who lives on the margins of conventional beauty."

—ERICKA HART

"

GIVE A GIRL AN
INSULT, SHE'LL
FEEL BAD FOR A
DAY, BUT TEACH A
GIRL TO HATE HER
BODY, SHE'LL FEEL
BAD FOREVER.

—JESSICA SIMPSON

"

"Boys have teased me about my curves since fifth grade. . . . In an era when so many women are stepping up to lead, I'm hoping people will focus on our ideas and accomplishments instead of our appearance. Until then, I've got a message for all of the women and girls like mine who have to deal with garbage like this every day: I've got your back."

—GOVERNOR GRETCHEN WHITMER

"My self in my most natural
form is my secret weapon.
It's my warrior garb."

—JENNY SLATE

My relationship with food was exactly the same psychology that I applied to everything else in my life: If I was given a pat on the head, I registered that as good. If I was given a punishment, I registered that as bad. . . . You register that enough times, and you just start to accommodate everything towards praise and punishment, including your own body.

—TAYLOR SWIFT

"BLACK IS BEAUTIFUL,
BUT IT TOOK ME A WHILE
TO SEE THE BEAUTY IN
MY BLACKNESS."

—NGOZI UFERE

"We have this default setting [of beauty] that's based off years and years of visual programming of seeing the exact same perfected bodies and faces. We all know that's not what humans look like in real life."

—BUSY PHILIPPS

IT'S SO EXHAUSTING
TO BE LIKE, 'I'M GOING
TO HATE MYSELF, ALL
THE TIME, FOREVER. . . .
EVERY TIME I GET
DRESSED. EVERY TIME
I GO TO DINNER. EVERY
TIME I DO ANYTHING.'

—AIDY BRYANT

"Even the existence of a plus-size section creates a boundary between us and 'regular' people. The term 'plus-size' is a misnomer. Who decides at what size a person stops being just a size and starts needing an entirely new category?"

—HEATHER JONES

"I . . . hope that for anyone who's been deemed 'other' to know that what makes you different, is your power, especially the unapologetic expression of your sexuality, gender, and the value of your unique perspective."

—GEENA ROCERO

Many Black women—
including myself—
know how much
baggage is associated
with our hair. So
much is assumed and
projected on how our
hair is worn.

—JESSICA MOULITE

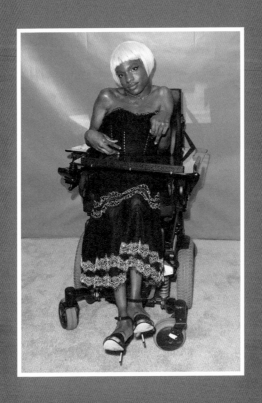

"I like my body enough to know that my body is and should be seen as chic, stylish, sexy, etc. as my disabled body."

—AARON PHILIP

"THIS IS YOUR COUNTRY, THIS IS YOUR WORLD, THIS IS YOUR BODY, AND YOU MUST FIND SOME WAY TO LIVE WITHIN THE ALL OF IT."

—TA-NEHISI COATES

"I'm fat. Full-figured. Thick.
Plus-size. Powerful. Capable.
Empowering. Phenomenal. . . .
I am powerful because I believe
that I am. And I owe nobody an
explanation for what moves me."

—LATOYA SHAUNTAY SNELL

If they don't have this idea that a disabled woman can be a romantic lead, you're not going to see that. Their idea of what should be on screen is so limited by what's been on screen, that their world isn't expanded to include people like me, and talent like me.

—DANIELLE PEREZ

Caring about one's appearance is far from being 'anti-feminist.' . . . It is a continuation of what feminism, in some ways, stands for: freedom of choice. Choosing to let our looks be one among other aspects of who we are as women is our right.

—VIVIAN DILLER, PHD

"I've spent my entire life feeling
like I'm captive inside my own
skin. I used to describe it when I
was younger, or I guess I still do,
as feeling like I'm covered in a
film. As if the imaginary layers
of fat that I feel all over me are
a thick suit that I want to rip off
every second of every day. . . .
Self-hatred is a powerful emotion."

—ZOSIA MAMET

"WOULD YOU LIKE ME TO BE SMALLER? WEAKER? SOFTER? TALLER? . . . AM I MY STOMACH, MY HIPS, THE BODY I WAS BORN WITH? . . . THOUGH YOU'VE NEVER SEEN MY BODY, YOU STILL JUDGE IT AND JUDGE ME FOR IT. WHY?"

—BILLIE EILISH

"NO MATTER HOW
HUGE, HOW INSANE,
HOW UNREASONABLE
OR UNREACHABLE YOUR
GOALS MAY SEEM,
NOTHING—NOT EVEN YOUR
OWN BODY—CAN HOLD
YOU BACK IF YOU ARE
CERTAIN AND FEARLESS
AND, YES, EVEN A LITTLE
BALLSY IN YOUR QUEST."

—JANET MOCK

"Sometimes I'm curious to know if I would have been as successful if I wasn't plus-size. I think I remind everyone of themselves. Not saying everyone is my size, but it's relatable because I'm not perfect, and I think a lot of people are portrayed as perfect, unreachable, and untouchable."

—ADELE

Your weight will fluctuate, your face will change. Nothing stays the same. But to actually not care about being— for lack of a better word—fuckable, to people and understanding that the only reason that when women are put under these pressures is for other people and not for themselves. . . . Once you unpack that and remove it from your life, you start understanding how much energy you wasted on it and how much more freedom you have without it.

—BARBIE FERREIRA

Can I honestly say that I've
had to face the same racism
and struggles as a woman with
darker skin? No, I cannot. . . .
But I'm completely behind that
woman. . . . And if I get put in
a position because of the color
of my skin where people will
listen to me, then I should use
that privilege the right way.

—ZENDAYA

"I have always tried to overcome the limitations of my condition and lead as full a life as possible . . . My advice to other disabled people would be, concentrate on things your disability doesn't prevent you doing well, and don't regret the things it interferes with. Don't be disabled in spirit, as well as physically."

—STEPHEN HAWKING

DOES BEAUTY EVEN
. . . HAVE TO BE
SOMETHING PHYSICAL,
OR CAN IT JUST BE
. . . THE WAY YOU
EXIST IN THE WORLD?

—JESI TAYLOR CRUZ

"I was very comfortable in my own skin, my sexuality, but it made the men uncomfortable. When it makes the men uncomfortable, it becomes your issue, which isn't fair."

—CARI CHAMPION

"Haven't we gotten past this? Can't we just see that you're a woman, you have light skin; I'm a woman, I have dark skin. We're both human. I can't wrap my head around the fact that people would treat someone different just because of how they look or their skin color. . . . I feel for those people because they're really just stuck."

—WILLOW SMITH

"YOUTH & BEAUTY R [SIC]
NOT ACCOMPLISHMENTS,
THEY'RE THE TEMPORARY
HAPPY B[Y]PRODUCTS
OF TIME &/OR DNA."

—CARRIE FISHER

"In my experience, you can't adequately explain to a two-year-old why beauty standards are largely based on long, straight-haired white women—or why she should be proud of her hair. . . . But you can surround that child with images and messages that expand notions of who and what we consider to be beautiful."

—MEENA HARRIS

I wish the world had encouraged
my fourteen-year-old self to
be more than just my body. . . .
Luckily I have discovered the
parts of me that are so much more
important than 'sexiness,' but if
you're a fourteen-year-old girl
reading this, don't worry about
any of that for now.

—EMILY RATAJKOWSKI

"When an adult white man asks me 'Where do you get your confidence?' the tacit assumption behind it is: 'Because you don't *look* like a person who should have any confidence. You're not white, you're not a man, and you're not thin or conventionally attractive. How were you able to overlook these obvious shortcomings to feel confident?'"

—MINDY KALING

This is my body. It is MINE. I am not ashamed of it in any way. In fact, I love everything about it. Men find it attractive. Clothes look awesome on it. My brain rides around in it all day and comes up with funny jokes. Also, I don't have to justify its awesomeness/attractiveness/healthiness/usefulness to anyone, because it is MINE. Not yours.

—LINDY WEST

"I don't want worrying about if I look hot or not on Instagram to be my legacy."

—COLTON HAYNES

He kept asking, 'Are you shocked that you actually work in this business at your tremendous size?' . . . I just remember all the blood drained out of me. I thought, 'With my tremendous size, I could tackle you so quickly.'

—MELISSA McCARTHY

"The world is so full of
culture—of diversity, of race,
of food, sounds, rhythm, body
shapes, just features—the
world is filled with so much,
and we're consistently just fed
this little bit."

—AMARA LA NEGRA

"We are relating to our bodies in different ways all of the time, and for some of us, we are continuing to create the language that truly speaks to how we exist in the world."

—TEXAS ISAIAH

Many of us are convinced that making women afraid to be fat is a form of social control. Fear of fat keeps women preoccupied, robs us of our pride and energy, keeps us from taking up space.

—BOSTON WOMEN'S
HEALTH BOOK COLLECTIVE

"OUR BODIES ARE OURS, OUR SEX APPEAL IS OURS, OUR KNOWLEDGE IS OURS. IT IS NOT OUR FAULT PEOPLE CAN'T HANDLE [OR] ARE NOT READY FOR IT. IT IS NOT OUR RESPONSIBILITY TO CARRY THAT BURDEN."

—ARIELLE CHAMBERS

Because your body is going to change, you have to deal with reality. And to deal with the reality, you have to know what you want and who you are. We come to it faster, women. Society has taught us this is negative.

—SANDRA OH

Loving your body is a choice
you make, and it's not up
to anyone else to validate or
tell you that you're beautiful
enough. It's up to you. You
hold that power, and when you
make that choice, nobody
can change it.

—ANASTASIA GARCIA

"AT SOME POINT, IT HIT
ME THAT ME AND MY
BODY ARE GOING TO HAVE
TO BE FRIENDS FOR A
LONG TIME, SO I BETTER
START TREATING IT LIKE
A FRIEND."

—JASON SEGEL

"I decided I wasn't going to FaceTune my body anymore. Instead of hiding it I'm going to be so unapologetic about this body and maybe if people see confidence they will be less likely to say mean things. Honestly something as simple as not FaceTuning out stretch marks felt like such a liberating act of protest."

—MINA GERGES

"Society is very afraid
of teenage girls and afraid of
sexuality amongst teenage
girls. People don't talk about it
because they're scared of it."

—BEL POWLEY

"I DON'T KNOW
WHY BUT OTHERS
FEEL AS THOUGH
THEY CAN
DEFINE YOUR
OWN BEAUTY
BASED ON THEIR
STANDARDS."

—SIMONE BILES

"I'm tired of talking about
my body with strangers.
Genuinely how can I stay
positive when I'm being
asked about being fat
every ten minutes?"

—CHIKA

The hair decisions afforded to Black women are inherently political. We decide to weave our hair and are accused of assimilating. We wear it natural or in braids and are praised for honoring our diaspora. The versatility of Black hair is a double-edged sword: great for the wearer but open for public scrutiny.

—NATASHA MARSH

"We should be allowed to make healthy choices publicly without being made to feel like frauds for trying to be healthy. I feel it's important to share the journey, as a reminder that we are not alone, we ain't always got it together, and that we are ALL works in progress."

—DANIELLE BROOKS

When I enter into a
relationship, I am not filling
a hole that society has dug out
of my soul, telling me that
I am fat, and because I am
fat I am ugly, and because I
am ugly I am unlovable. . . .
I am not seeking validation
from a partner, I am seeking
partnership in that partner.

—ALITHEA O'DELL

"I ran for governor as a sturdy woman with natural hair, a gap between my teeth . . . and because I like who I am and because I knew I was the best person for the job, I wasn't going to wait until Weight Watchers or Jenny Craig turned me into the 'after' picture; I wasn't going to Invisalign myself out of looking like my mother. . . . I want to be healthy, but I'm not trying to fit anyone else's image, because there has not been what I am. Therefore, I'm going to be what I am."

—STACEY ABRAMS

# "DARK-SKINNED WOMEN ARE ALWAYS KIND OF AT THE BOTTOM OF THE TOTEM POLE. I DON'T UNDERSTAND THAT."

## —JACKIE AINA

"This is for every guy built with some extra meat, that unbuttons that bottom button when tryna avoid the crease, that has to shop around like crazy cause the sizes for us are already gone but we sauce up a fit and still flex the drip. We here, we are sexy, and we are the wave."

—STEVEN G

"HAIRSTYLES BECOME
A WAY IN WHICH AN
IDENTITY OR POLITICS
ARE PLACED ON
BLACK WOMEN'S
BODIES, WHETHER WE
ASCRIBE TO THOSE
POLITICS OR NOT."

—INGRID BANKS

"I have a deep voice,
I don't have boobs. . . .
It's OK. . . . It does not
change that I'm a woman."

—CASTER SEMENYA

"I'M A BLACK WOMAN IN AMERICA. AND YOU KNOW, WE'RE NOT ALWAYS MADE TO FEEL BEAUTIFUL. SO THERE'S STILL THAT BAGGAGE THAT WE CARRY, AND NOT EVERYONE CAN RELATE TO THAT."

—MICHELLE OBAMA

66

The problem with today's
version of body positivity is that it
refuses to acknowledge that
no one approach is right for every
person. . . . I've come to feel
that loving yourself and desiring
to change yourself are two
sentiments that should be able to
peacefully coexist.

—KELLY DEVOS

99

"You're meant to be you, you're meant to be in this body. It's your home, so if you can start loving and respecting it, then that to me is the beginning of confidence."

—ISKRA LAWRENCE

# BIOGRAPHIES

**STACEY ABRAMS** *(she/her)* is an attorney, voting rights activist, author, former Minority Leader of the Georgia House of Representatives and 2018 Georgia gubernatorial candidate. As founder of the Fair Fight Action voting initiative, Abrams has been widely credited with galvanizing voter turnout and turning Georgia in favor of the Democratic party for the first time since the 1990s.

**JAYDE ADAMS** *(she/her)* is a British comedian, singer, and television personality recently seen on Amazon Prime's *Good Omens* and as the host of *Crazy Delicious* on Netflix.

**ADELE** *(she/her)* is a British-born singer-songwriter who has won multiple Grammy Awards.

**JACKIE AINA** *(she/her)* is a YouTube beauty content creator, entrepreneur, and advocate for representation for darker-skinned women in the beauty and fashion industries.

**INGRID BANKS** *(she/her)* is Associate Professor of Black Studies at the University of California Santa Barbara and author of the book *Hair Matters: Beauty, Power, and Black Women's Consciousness*.

**SIMONE BILES** *(she/her)* is the most decorated American and the world's third most decorated gymnast of any gender, having won a combined total of thirty Olympic and World Championship medals. She is also the namesake of several complex gymnastics maneuvers.

**ALEX BORSTEIN** *(she/her)* is an actress, writer, comedian, and producer. She provided the voice of Lois on *Family Guy*, and has won two Emmy Awards for the role of Susie Myerson on Netflix's *The Marvelous Mrs. Maisel*.

**BOSTON WOMEN'S HEALTH BOOK COLLECTIVE** is the feminist group that authored *Our Bodies, Ourselves* at the height of the women's liberation movement. They also wrote its successors: *Changing Bodies, Changing Lives: A Book for Teens on Sex and Relationships*; *The New Ourselves, Growing Older: Women Aging with Knowledge and Power*; *Our Bodies, Ourselves: Menopause*; and *Our Bodies, Ourselves: Pregnancy and Birth*.

**DANIELLE BROOKS** *(she/her)* is a Tony-nominated actress and singer known for her role in *The Color Purple: The Musical* on Broadway, and her series regular role in Netflix's *Orange Is the New Black*.

**KEAH BROWN** *(she/her)* is an author, journalist, disability rights activist, and creator of the hashtag #DisabledAndCute. Her first book, *The Pretty One: On Life, Pop Culture, Disability, and Other Reasons to Fall in Love with Me*, was published in 2019.

**SHERRONDA J. BROWN** *(she/they)* is an essayist, editor, academic, and digital activist whose work explores media, social issues, and pop culture through a Black feminist lens.

**AIDY BRYANT** *(she/her)* is an actress and comedian best known as a cast member of *Saturday Night Live*, for which she has been nominated for two Primetime Emmy Awards. Bryant is also the star of Hulu's *Shrill*, adapted from Lindy West's memoir of the same name.

**LILLIAN BUSTLE** *(she/her)* is a burlesque performer, singer, emcee, and public speaker whose TEDx Talk, "Stripping Away Negative Body Image," focused on the self-affirming aspects of burlesque.

**LYNDA CARTER** *(she/her)* is an actress, singer, songwriter, and model best known for her role as Diana Prince on the television show *Wonder Woman*. Carter was also crowned Miss World USA in 1972.

**MAMA CAX** *(she/her)* was a model, blogger, influencer, and disability advocate. After losing most of her right leg to cancer in her teens, Mama Cax ultimately found unexpected success as a top model with her prosthesis on full display, making appearances for Savage X Fenty, Tommy Hilfiger, Maison Margiela, and more.

**ARIELLE CHAMBERS** *(she/her)* is a multimedia journalist, social media manager, model, and creator and voice of "HighlightHER," the Bleacher Report's women's platform. A member of the Forbes "30 Under 30" Class of 2021, Chambers covers the Women's National Basketball Association (WNBA), the National Collegiate Athletic Association (NCAA), and the Atlantic Coast Conference (ACC).

**CARI CHAMPION** *(she/her)* is a sports journalist, television personality, and former ESPN anchor who cohosts Vice on TV's *Cari & Jemele (Won't) Stick to Sports*.

**DAVE CHAWNER** *(he/him)* is a British-born comedian, bestselling author, and mental health advocate. His TED Talk on eating disorders led to the publication of a memoir, *Weight Expectations*.

**CHIKA** *(she/her)* is a Grammy-nominated rapper, actress, and model.

**TA-NEHISI COATES** *(he/him)* is a journalist, author, and thought leader renowned for his writing on race and class in America. The recipient of a MacArthur Fellowship, Coates has authored numerous bestsellers including *The Beautiful Struggle*, *We Were Eight Years in Power*, and *Between the World and Me*, which was adapted into a stage performance and HBO special. Coates also authored two series for Marvel Comics, including several issues of *Black Panther*.

**NICOLA COUGHLAN** *(she/her)* is an Irish actress who has appeared in the sitcom *Derry Girls* and as Penelope Featherington in the hit Netflix period drama *Bridgerton*.

**JESI TAYLOR CRUZ** *(she/they)* is an environmental justice consultant and staff writer for *Romper*, reporting on issues of race, politics, and identity.

**KELLY DEVOS** *(she/her)* is a body-positive journalist and YA author whose debut novel, *Fat Girl on a Plane*, was named one of the "50 Best Summer Reads of All Time" by *Reader's Digest* magazine.

**VIVIAN DILLER, PHD** *(she/her)* is a New York City–based psychologist, media expert, and marketing consultant.

**PETER DINKLAGE** *(he/him)* is an Emmy- and Golden Globe–winning actor, producer, and musician best known for *The Station Agent* and his starring role as Tyrion Lannister in HBO's *Game of Thrones*.

**WARIS DIRIE** *(she/her)* is a Somali-born model, author, actress, human rights activist, and former UN special ambassador against female genital mutilation, fighting to outlaw the practice through her Desert Flower Foundation.

**CHIZI DURU** *(she/her)* is a model, actress, and YouTube creator and influencer.

**BILLIE EILISH** *(she/her)* is a singer-songwriter who made Grammy Award history as the youngest person and second person to win the four main categories (Best New Artist, Record of the Year, Song of the Year, and Album of the Year) in the same year.

**BEANIE FELDSTEIN** *(she/her)* is a Golden Globe–nominated actress and singer who has appeared in the films *Lady Bird* and *Booksmart*, as well as the Broadway revival of *Hello, Dolly!*, and the comedy series *What We Do in the Shadows*.

**BARBIE FERREIRA** *(she/her)* is an actress and model best known as a series regular on HBO's *Euphoria*.

**CARRIE FISHER** *(she/her)* was an actress and author, known for her portrayal of Princess Leia in the *Star Wars* franchise and for roles in numerous other films, including *The Blues Brothers*, *Hannah and Her Sisters*, and *When Harry Met Sally*. Fisher also wrote several acclaimed books, including the semi-autobiographical *Postcards From the Edge*, adapted into a film, and a memoir, *Wishful Drinking*, which was adapted into a one-woman show starring Fisher on Broadway.

**ALLIE FLYNN** *(she/her)* is a beauty and wellness writer whose work has appeared in publications including Well+Good, the Zoe Report, Brides, Bustle, Greatist, PopSugar, and HelloGiggles.

**JANE FONDA** *(she/her)* is an Emmy-, Golden Globe–, BAFTA-, and Academy Award–winning actress, producer, political and environmental activist, and former model and fitness personality. Her multidecade career includes acclaimed performances in *Barefoot in the Park*, *Klute*, *On Golden Pond*, and the Netflix series *Grace and Frankie*.

**STEVEN G** *(he/him)* is a photographer, creative director, and big and tall style expert best known for appearing as a model in a campaign for Savage X Fenty.

**HANNAH GADSBY** *(she/her)* is an Australian comedian, writer, actress, and television personality best known for her highly acclaimed 2018 Netflix stand-up special, *Nanette.*

**ANASTASIA GARCIA** *(she/her)* is a New York–based photographer, writer, and advocate for body diversity and representation in fashion.

**ROXANE GAY** *(she/her)* is a writer, professor, editor, and thought leader whose published works include the bestselling *Bad Feminist* and her memoir, *Hunger.*

**MINA GERGES** *(he/him)* is a plus-size male model, influencer, and body positive advocate who has appeared in campaigns for Calvin Klein and Sephora. Gerges's mission is to "redefine unrealistic beauty standards in the fashion world."

**SELENA GOMEZ** *(she/her)* is a singer, actress, and producer who first gained popularity on the Disney series *Wizards of Waverly Place,* and has since garnered acclaim for several platinum-selling albums. Also an entrepreneur, Gomez's most recent venture was the launch of the inclusive and instantly successful Rare Beauty.

**TIM GUNN** *(he/him)* is a fashion consultant, designer, television personality, and author of several books. He was the talent mentor on *Project Runway* while also serving as chair of Fashion Design at Parsons School of Design.

**WINNIE HARLOW** *(she/her)* is a Jamaican Canadian fashion model and spokesperson who rose to acclaim as the first *America's Next Top Model* contestant and later supermodel with the skin condition vitiligo.

**MEENA HARRIS** *(she/her)* is an attorney, children's book author, producer, and founder of the Phenomenal Woman Action Campaign, which brings awareness to social causes via its often-viral T-shirts. Harris also served as a senior adviser on the presidential campaign of her aunt, Vice President Kamala Harris.

**ERICKA HART** *(she/they)* is a professor, activist, sex educator, and model, recognized in *The Root* 100 Class of 2018 as an "advocate for post-cancer body positivity."

**STEPHEN HAWKING** *(he/him)* was a British-born theoretical physicist and cosmologist best known for authoring the international bestseller *A Brief History of Time.* Diagnosed with the motor neuron disease ALS while earning his doctorate in his early twenties, Hawking's findings on relativity and quantum mechanics ultimately earned him the Presidential Medal of Freedom, the highest civilian award in the United States.

**SALMA HAYEK** *(she/her)* is an Emmy-, Golden Globe–, and Academy Award–nominated actress, screenwriter, and producer. Born in Mexico, she is acclaimed for her starring performance as Frida Kahlo in *Frida,* which she also produced.

**COLTON HAYNES** *(he/him)* is an actor and model, best known for his series regular role as Arsenal on the CW's *Arrow*.

**JONAH HILL** *(he/him)* is an Academy Award–nominated actor, director, producer, screenwriter, and comedian known for his roles in the films *Superbad*, *Moneyball*, and *The Wolf of Wall Street*, among others. Hill is also the creator of the zine *Inner Children*, a collection of celebrity essays and musings on childhood.

**SAMANTHA IRBY** *(she/her)* is a comedian, blogger, and author of the essay collections *Meaty*; *We Are Never Meeting in Real Life*; *New Year, Same Trash*; and *Wow, No Thank You*.

**TEXAS ISAIAH** *(he/they)* is a Black Indigenous American photographer and contemporary artist.

**JAZZ JENNINGS** *(she/her)* is a television personality, model, and LGBTQ rights advocate whose story has been chronicled on TLC's *I Am Jazz*.

**HEATHER JONES** *(she/her)* is a writer focusing on parenting, diversity, and social change.

**MINDY KALING** *(she/her)* is an actress, comedian, screenwriter, producer, director, and author known for her on- and offscreen work on *The Office*, *The Mindy Project*, Hulu's series reboot of *Four Weddings and a Funeral*, and the films *A Wrinkle in Time* and *Ocean's 8*.

**NORMA KAMALI** *(she/her)* is a fashion designer, author, and wellness advocate. Kamali famously designed both the red swimsuit Farrah Fawcett wore in the popular 1976 poster and the iconic sleeping bag coat. She is the author of *I Am Invincible*, and a winner of the Council of Fashion Designers of America's Geoffrey Beene Lifetime Achievement Award.

**KELLY KNOX** *(she/her)* is a British fashion model, TV personality, and activist. Born without a left forearm, she has refused to wear a prosthesis since childhood.

**PHILOMENA KWAO** *(she/her)* is a British Ghanaian model, influencer, and advocate for maternal health and women's rights, as well as an outspoken advocate for color and size diversity in fashion and beauty.

**AMA KWARTENG** *(she/her)* is the associate beauty editor at both the print and digital editions of *Cosmopolitan* magazine.

**AMARA LA NEGRA** *(she/her)* is a Dominican American singer, actress, dancer, author, and television host, known for her role on VH1's *Love & Hip Hop: Miami*.

**ISKRA LAWRENCE** *(she/her)* is a British plus-sized model, body positivity advocate and brand ambassador for L'Oréal and Aerie, among others.

**LIZZO** *(she/her)* is a Grammy Award–winning singer-songwriter, rapper, and flutist named *Time*'s "Entertainer of the Year" for 2019. She has also earned film credits in 2019's *Hustlers* and *Ugly Dolls*.

**DEMI LOVATO** *(they/them)* is a Grammy-nominated and platinum-selling singer-songwriter and actor.

**ZOSIA MAMET** *(she/her)* is an actress, writer, and musician. She has appeared in roles on *Mad Men* and as a series regular on *Girls* and *The Flight Attendant*.

**ANTHONY PATRICK MANIERI** *(he/him)* is a Toronto-based photographer, art director, and creator of the male-focused nude portrait series *Arrested Movement*.

**MEGHAN MARKLE** *(she/her)* is an actress, producer, humanitarian, and member of the British royal family. She was formerly the duchess of Sussex.

**NATASHA MARSH** *(she/her)* is a writer covering fashion, beauty, and lifestyle. Based in New York City but raised in California, she held styling staff positions at the *Wall Street Journal*, Burberry, *Cosmopolitan*, *British GQ*, and *Harper's Bazaar*.

**MELISSA McCARTHY** *(she/her)* is an Emmy-winning and Golden Globe– and Academy Award–nominated actress, comedian, writer, producer, and fashion designer, known for her work in the television series *Mike & Molly* and the films *Bridesmaids*, *Tammy*, and *Can You Ever Forgive Me?*, among others.

**SHOOG McDANIEL** *(they/them)* is a queer, nonbinary, and body-positive photographer and artist based in Tallahassee, Florida.

**JILLIAN MERCADO** *(she/her)* is an actress, activist, and fashion model represented by CAA (Creative Artists Agency). Diagnosed with muscular dystrophy in childhood, Mercado is also the founder of Black Disabled Creatives, launched "to help bridge the divide for Black creatives with disabilities."

**ZACH MIKO** *(he/him)* is an actor, writer, and model who came to national recognition as the first-ever "Brawn" model signed to IMG Models.

**JANET MOCK** *(she/her)* is a bestselling author, journalist, television personality, director, producer, and transgender rights activist who made television history as the first transgender woman of color to write and direct any television episode. She is also the first to ink a first-look development deal with a major content company (Netflix).

**INDYA MOORE** *(they/them)* is a model, actress, and LGBTQ advocate, best known for their role as Angel Evangelista in FX's *Pose*.

**JESSICA MOULITE** *(she/her)* is a Webby Award–winning video producer and journalist at *The Root*.

**AIMEE MULLINS** *(she/her)* is an athlete, actress, model, and public speaker. Born with a medical condition that required the amputation of both of her lower legs, Mullins was the first female amputee in history to compete in the NCAA, and the first amputee to compete in NCAA Division I track and field. She also competed in the 1996 Paralympic Games.

**HARI NEF** *(she/her)* is a SAG Award–nominated actress, model, and writer, best known for her role as Gittel in *Transparent*.

**LUPITA NYONG'O** *(she/her)* is an Academy Award–winning actress and children's book author who has been an outspoken advocate on the impact of colorism on children and popular culture.

**MICHELLE OBAMA** *(she/her)* is an attorney, producer, podcast host, voting and human rights advocate, bestselling author of 2018's *Becoming*, and former first lady of the United States.

**ALITHEA O'DELL** *(she/her)* is a printmaker and letterpress printer based in Olympia, Washington.

**SANDRA OH** *(she/her)* is a Golden Globe–winning and Emmy-nominated actress best known for her starring roles on the series *Arliss*, *Grey's Anatomy*, and *Killing Eve*, as well as her performances in films such as *Sideways* and *Under the Tuscan Sun*, among others.

**MATT ORTILE** *(he/him)* is a New York–based journalist and author of the essay collection *The Groom Will Keep His Name*. He is the managing editor of *Catapult* magazine. He also was the founding editor of BuzzFeed Philippines.

**DOLLY PARTON** *(she/her)* is a celebrated singer-songwriter, multi-instrumentalist, actress, author, entrepreneur, and humanitarian. An inductee into the Country Music Hall of Fame, Parton's accolades include ten Grammy Awards, including the Lifetime Achievement Award, ten Country Music Association Awards, and three American Music Awards.

**DANIELLE PEREZ** *(she/her)* is a stand-up comedian, actor, and writer.

**BUSY PHILIPPS** *(she/her)* is an actress and television personality known for her roles on *Dawson's Creek*, *ER*, and *Cougar Town*. Philipps has numerous film credits and also hosted her own late-night talk show on the E! Network, *Busy Tonight*.

**AARON PHILLIP** *(she/her)* is a fashion model and author. Diagnosed with cerebral palsy in infancy, she has since become widely known as the first Black, transgender, and physically disabled model to ever be represented by a major modeling agency (Elite Models). She is a model and muse for major designers like Marc Jacobs, Jeremy Scott, and Moschino, as well as fashion publications like *American Vogue*, *British Vogue*, and *Vogue Italia*.

**P!NK** *(she/her)* is a Grammy-winning and platinum-selling singer-songwriter named one of the "100 Greatest Women in Music" by VH1.

**NATALIE PORTMAN** *(she/her)* is an Academy Award– and Golden Globe–winning actress and filmmaker known for her work in the films *Léon: The Professional*, *V for Vendetta*, *Closer*, *Black Swan*, and *Jackie*, among others.

**BEL POWLEY** *(she/her)* is an award-winning British-born actress known for her starring role in the coming-of-age film *The Diary of a Teenage Girl*; she has also appeared in Apple TV+'s *The Morning Show*.

**ALY RAISMAN** *(she/her)* is a retired gymnast and two-time Olympian who was captain of both the 2012 and 2016 gold medal–winning US women's Olympic gymnastics teams.

**Dᴀ'VINE JOY RANDOLPH** *(she/her)* is a Tony-nominated actress and singer known for her roles in Broadway's *Ghost: The Musical*, the film *Dolemite Is My Name*, and Hulu's *High Fidelity*.

**EMILY RATAJKOWSKI** *(she/her)* is a model, actress, and spokesperson for Planned Parenthood.

**GEENA ROCERO** *(she/her)* is a model, trans activist, and founder of Gender Proud, a media production company centering trans voices and visibility. In the midst of a successful modeling career, Rocero chose to reveal that she was transgender on the Transgender Day of Visibility 2014 during a highly acclaimed TED Talk.

**ANGELICA ROSS** *(she/her)* is an actress, entrepreneur, and transgender rights advocate. She is best known for her back-to-back series regular roles in FX's *Pose* and *American Horror Story: 1984*. Ross is also the founder and CEO of TransTech Social Enterprises, a training and advocacy organization.

**TRACEE ELLIS ROSS** *(she/her)* is an Emmy-nominated and Golden Globe–winning actress, producer, director, singer, and beauty entrepreneur best known for her costarring roles on *Girlfriends* and *Black-ish*, as well as the 2020 film *The High Note*. Ellis Ross is also the founder of the haircare brand Pattern Beauty.

**NATASHA ROTHWELL** *(she/her)* is an actress, comedian, writer, and producer. A former writer for *Saturday Night Live*, Rothwell plays series regular Kelli on *Insecure*, where she is also writer and supervising producer.

**HUNTER SCHAFER** *(she/her)* is a model, actress, and LGBTQ advocate who played Jules in HBO's *Euphoria*.

**AMY SCHUMER** *(she/her)* is an Emmy-, Tony-, Grammy-, and Golden Globe–nominated actress, comedian, bestselling author, and producer. She starred in the Comedy Central series *Inside Amy Schumer*, and the films *Trainwreck* and *I Feel Pretty*.

**JASON SEGEL** *(he/him)* is an actor, comedian, screenwriter, singer-songwriter, author, and producer. He was a series regular on *How I Met Your Mother*, and has appeared in films including *Forgetting Sarah Marshall*, *The Five-Year Engagement*, and *The End of the Tour*.

**CASTER SEMENYA** *(she/her)* is a South African middle-distance runner and 2016 Olympic gold medalist who was named one of *Time* magazine's 100 Most Influential People of 2019.

**JESSICA SIMPSON** *(she/her)* is a singer, actress, fashion entrepreneur, television personality, and bestselling author.

**JENNY SLATE** *(she/her)* is an actress, comedian, and author known for her performances in the Showtime series *House of Lies*, the film *Obvious Child*, and voice performances in animated films *The LEGO Batman Movie*, *Zootopia*, *The Secret Life of Pets*, and the series *Bob's Burgers*, among others.

**SAM SMITH** *(they/them)* is a British-born Grammy-, Golden Globe–, and Academy Award–winning nonbinary singer-songwriter, known for their hits "Stay With Me," "Too Good at Goodbyes," and the Bond theme "Writing's on the Wall," among others.

**WILLOW SMITH** *(she/her)* is a musician, actress, model, and television personality known for her hit single "Whip My Hair" and as a cohost on the Facebook series *Red Table Talk*.

**LATOYA SHAUNTAY SNELL** *(she/her)* is a chef, writer, photographer, runner, and body-positive activist whose 2017 essay for *The Root*, "I'm a Plus-Size Runner and I Got Heckled at the NYC Marathon," went viral.

**MEGAN THEE STALLION** *(she/her)* is a Grammy-nominated rapper, model, and singer-songwriter named one of 2020's "100 Most Influential People in the World" by *Time* magazine.

**JESSAMYN STANLEY** *(she/her)* is a yoga instructor, body positivity advocate, and author of *Every Body Yoga: Let Go of Fear, Get On the Mat, Love Your Body*. As a public figure, Stanley has been largely credited with increasingly inclusivity in American yoga culture.

**TAYLOR SWIFT** *(she/her)* is a multi-platinum and Grammy- and Emmy Award–winning singer-songwriter, instrumentalist, and actress, recognized on several prominent lists as one of the greatest music artists of her generation.

**ANDRÉ LEON TALLEY** *(he/him)* is a fashion journalist, former editor-at-large for *American Vogue*, and the author of several books, including a bestselling memoir, *The Chiffon Trenches*, published in 2020.

**NYMA TANG** *(she/her)* is a YouTube beauty content creator and influencer whose series *The Darkest Shade* positioned her as an activist for greater shade representation for darker skin tones in beauty products.

**SONYA RENEE TAYLOR** *(she/her)* is a poet and spoken word artist; public speaker; human, social justice and body activist; and educator. She is the founder of The Body Is Not an Apology movement and the author of a book of the same name.

**NGOZI UFERE** *(she/her)* is the deputy editor at *Pride Magazine Nigeria*.

**LINDA WELLS** *(she/her)* is a journalist, the founder and former editor-in-chief of *Allure* magazine, and creator of the cosmetic brand Flesh.

**LINDY WEST** *(she/her)* is a comedian, activist, journalist, and author of the bestselling memoir *Shrill: Notes from a Loud Woman*. She is also an executive producer and writer for the Hulu series of the same name.

**GOVERNOR GRETCHEN WHITMER** *(she/her)* is a Democratic politician who has served as the governor of Michigan since 2019, prior to which she served in both Michigan's House of Representatives and Senate.

**ALICE WONG** *(she/her)* is a disability activist. Born with muscular dystrophy, Wong is the founder and project coordinator of the Disability Visibility Project (DVP), a collaboration with StoryCorps centering the oral histories of people with disabilities in the US.

**JAMILA WOODS** *(she/her)* is a Chicago-based singer-songwriter and poet whose work focuses on Black feminism, legacy, self-care, and advocacy.

**MALCOLM X** *(he/him)* was an activist and one of the most influential leaders of the civil rights movement and the Nation of Islam. He was assassinated in 1965, but his stature only grew, particularly after the publication of his bestselling book, *The Autobiography of Malcolm X*.

**ZENDAYA** *(she/her)* is an Emmy-winning actress, singer, model, and producer who was first recognized for her performances on the Disney sitcoms *Shake It Up* and *K. C. Undercover*, where she played the titular role of K. C. Cooper. After releasing several albums and also appearing in *The Greatest Showman* and multiple installments of the *Spider-Man* franchise, Zendaya became the youngest actor to win a Primetime Emmy for her role as Rue in HBO's *Euphoria*, which she also produces.

# PHOTO CREDITS

# ACKNOWLEDGMENTS

Deep gratitude to Sharyn Rosart, publisher of Spruce Books, for trusting me with this most intimate of topics for this incredible series—and for limitless patience and guidance through the process. Thanks are also due to the impeccable eye of production editor Jill Saginario, designers Alison Keefe and Alicia Terry, and photo researcher Jennifer Rudsit for beautifully bringing these words to life. To Tanya McKinnon and Carol Taylor of McKinnon Literary, thank you for your advocacy, believing in my voice, and for sealing the deal—you are the best. Thanks to Danielle Belton, my former editor-in-chief, for recommending me for this project and giving me such an expansive platform at *The Root*. To Gary Dakin and the extended family at JAG Models, thank you for believing in my body, and empowering me to be part of the first wave of what has become the body positivity movement. To my mother, Patricia Arnold, thank you for always giving first eyes to my work. To the Simpsons, Greens, and day-ones, your unconditional support is everything. To my love, thank you for loving whatever body I'm in.

Printed in China

SPRUCE BOOKS with colophon is a registered trademark
of Penguin Random House LLC

26 25 24 23 22                    9 8 7 6 5 4 3 2 1

Editor: Sharyn Rosart
Production editor: Jill Saginario
Designers: Alison Keefe and Alicia Terry
Photo researcher: Jennifer Rudsit

Library of Congress Cataloging-in-Publication Data is available.

**FOR A FULL LIST OF CITATIONS FOR EACH QUOTE APPEARING IN
THIS BOOK, PLEASE VISIT MAIYSHA.COM.**

ISBN: 978-1-63217-406-2

Spruce Books, a Sasquatch Books Imprint
1904 Third Avenue, Suite 710
Seattle, WA 98101

SasquatchBooks.com

# LOOK FOR OTHER TITLES IN THE
# WORDS OF CHANGE SERIES

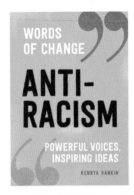

**SPRUCE BOOKS**

A Sasquatch Books Imprint

**MAIYSHA KAI** is a journalist, style expert, voice-over artist and Grammy-nominated vocalist with over two decades of industry experience both on camera and off, representing beauty and fashion brands as a model, spokesperson, and body image advocate. She is currently the managing editor of lifestyle content at the leading Black news and opinion site *The Root*, where she also hosts and produces the *It's Lit!* literary podcast.